THE SQUARE MILE

THE SQUARE MILE

A PHOTOGRAPHIC PORTRAIT OF THE CITY

Beata Moore

FRANCES LINCOLN LIMITED
PUBLISHERS

FOR MY SON, KONRAD

Frances Lincoln Ltd
4 Torriano Mews
Torriano Avenue
London NW5 2RZ
www.franceslincoln.com

The Square Mile
Copyright © Frances Lincoln Ltd 2010
Text and photographs copyright © Beata Moore 2010

First Frances Lincoln edition 2010

A catalogue record for this book is available from the British Library.

ISBN 978-0-7112-3027-9

Printed and bound in China

Contents

Introduction

The City of London refers to the area within the original old walled city built by the Romans around AD 50. This oldest part of London stretches from The Temple and Fleet Street to the west, Smithfield and the Barbican to the north, Aldgate and the Tower of London to the east and the River Thames to the south. This small area of approximately one square mile at the tidal limit of the Thames is the smallest ceremonial county in the country and a thriving business centre.

There were some settlements around the site of the city before Roman times, but the first reference to the city dates from AD 60, when 'Londinium' is mentioned by the historian Tacitus as an important centre of commerce. In AD 61 the city was burned to the ground by Queen Boudica of the Iceni tribe of East Anglia, who launched the rebellion against the Romans. As a result, the Romans surrounded the city with walls more than two metres high, which defended London for many centuries to come. The Romans ruled until AD 410, but when the troops left the area, London fell into obscurity. Later on in the same century, Anglo-Saxons settled here. The ninth century brought several invasions by Danish Vikings, followed by resettling in AD 883 by Alfred the Great, who recaptured London from the Danes and appointed Ethelred the governor of London. Under the Saxons, London became the metropolis of the Essex Kingdom. Since then, the area of the City of London has been administered separately.

Following the Battle of Hastings, William the Conqueror marched on London. His army never managed to cross London Bridge, but to avoid continuing the war, the city surrendered and was rewarded by the King with a charter that contained special privileges for Londoners, creating the basis of its autonomous status that continues to this day. In 1132, Henry I recognised the full county status of the City, and in 1191 Richard I acknowledged the right of London to self-governance. King John granted several more charters and confirmed all ancient privileges for the citizens of London, as well as the right for the citizens to choose their own Lord Mayor in the Magna Carta of 1215. The City steadily grew in size and prominence during the Middle Ages, and by the reign of the Stuarts, London had become a wealthy and successful city, in spite of frequent plagues and fires. The City was nearly burned to the ground twice, in 1212 and later in the Great Fire of London in 1666. Many historic buildings, 87 churches, St Paul's Cathedral, 44 companies' halls and over 13,000 buildings were completely destroyed. Sir Christopher Wren was commissioned to rebuild the City. Some wider streets were

◁ The City dragon near Tower Hill.

▽ Statue of the Roman Emperor Trajan at Tower Hill.

planned, but very innovative, grand-scale plans by Wren were never executed in their entirety. Following the rebuild and a rapid growth of the population, the City in the seventeenth and eighteenth centuries grew into the world's leading commercial and financial centre, with such lavish civic buildings as the Mansion House, the Royal Exchange and the Bank of England. Yet in the nineteenth century the City's population rapidly declined due to poor sanitary conditions, and as people started to move to healthier suburbs in the twentieth century. German bombing raids throughout the Second World War left much of the City in rubble. Some of the most valuable buildings were rebuilt after the war, while others were replaced with modern office blocks.

Most of the Roman and later medieval walls disappeared throughout the centuries, but the area of the City has not changed significantly. Its boundaries are marked with black bollards and monuments adorned with dragons. Originally the City had large gates at strategic points along the wall. These were: Temple Bar, Holborn, Aldersgate, Bishopsgate, Ludgate, Newgate, Cripplegate, Aldgate and Moorgate. Built to collect tolls and for safety, they were demolished at the end of the eighteenth century.

The City of London is administered by the City of London Corporation and headed by the Lord Mayor of London. The City is home to the Bank of England, the London Stock Exchange, more than 200 banks, hundreds of financial institutions, as well as City of London Corporation and Lord Mayor's Mansion. The motto of the City is 'Domine, dirige nos' (Lord, guide us). The City to this day guards its ancient rights and prerogatives. Its electoral system is unique, as most voters represent businesses established in the City.

Commerce in the City was traditionally managed by Livery Companies, which descended from medieval guilds. They provided training and welfare for their members and regulated their trades. Over the years they reached considerable power, grew rich and built elaborate halls in which guests and members were entertained. Unfortunately many of the Livery Halls were destroyed either in the Great Fire or during the Second World War. There are 108 Livery Companies, almost all of them known as 'Worshipful Companies'. They remain living institutions, but most of them are charitable organisations, promoting the professions, supporting education

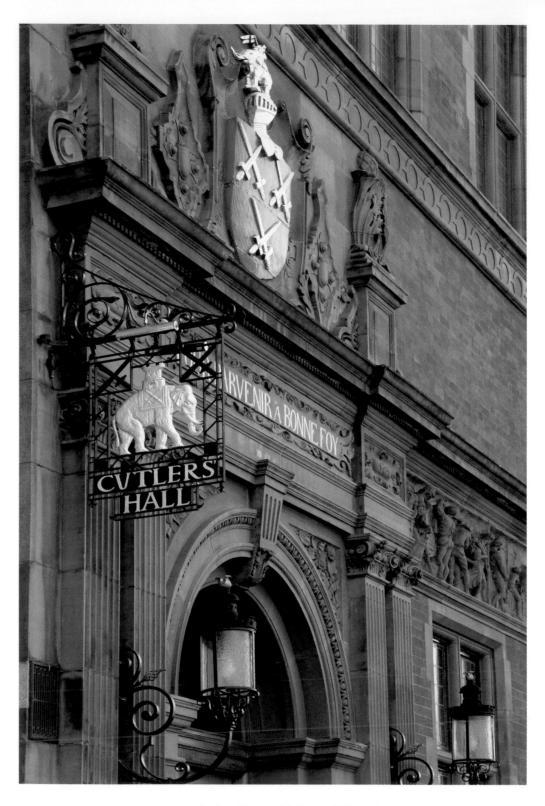

Cutlers' Livery Hall at 4 Warwick Lane.

Barclays Office at Lombard Street and Tower 42 at Old Broad Street.

and carrying out important functions in the election of the government. All of them have traditional customs handed down for generations and on special occasions members wear a distinctive dress.

The Right Honourable Lord Mayor of London presides over City of London governing bodies, the Court of Alderman and the Court of Common Council. Each Lord Mayor serves for one year and one of his many duties is to promote the British Financial Sector. Elected at the 'Silent Ceremony' in November each year by Common Hall and all Liverymen of the City's Livery Companies, after taking office, he travels to the Royal Court of Justice to swear his allegiance to the Crown. This journey has been made for 784 years; it originated to show the New Lord Mayor to the people. Over the years it has been transformed into the famous Lord Mayor Show, containing traditional British pageantry and elements of carnival.

Local government services are provided by the City of London Corporation, which promotes the City and enhances its status as the world's leading business centre. It runs its own police force and the Central Criminal Court, the Old Bailey. The Guildhall as the headquarters of the City of London Corporation is in the heart of the City. It is here, in the Great Hall, that state and civic banquets, meetings of the Corporation's elected assembly, the Court of Common Council and the Honorary Freedom of the City ceremony are held.

The City embodies the mix of tradition and change; it is the most historic part of London, yet also the most modern, embracing Roman ruins, medieval timber buildings, Tudor and Georgian houses as well as iconic towering skyscrapers. Buildings such as the futuristic 'Darth Vader's Helmet' at Walbrook Square and the 'Walkie Talkie' at Fenchurch Street will soon change the iconic London skyline yet again and create an even more extraordinary juxtaposition of ancient and modern. It was a long process of change from the small trading centre protected by the Romans to the commercial and financial powerhouse of London. A kingdom of its own with many customs, traditions and pomp and ceremony preserved for centuries mixing easily with totally modern life style. A vibrant art and cultural environment that goes hand in hand with peaceful contemplation of the countless churches and tranquillity of green gems, gardens dotting the whole area of the City.

Sion Hall and the old City of London School.

St Paul's Cathedral from the London Millennium Footbridge.

Blackfriars Bridge.

From Victoria Embankment to Smithfield Market

THE VICTORIA EMBANKMENT

Victoria Embankment runs from the City of Westminster to Blackfriars Bridge in the City of London. Designed by Joseph Bazalgette, and constructed by the Metropolitan Board of Works in 1870, this colossal road and walkway was created on 52 acres of reclaimed riverside ground. The Embankment is embellished with traditional cast-iron lamp posts with dolphin bases, and seats adorned with camels. These have survived well since the Victorian era.

THE MIDDLE TEMPLE HALL

Located between Fleet Street and the Thames, the Inner and Middle Temples are two independent enclaves in the City, not governed by the City of London Corporation. They were originally the properties of the Knights Templar. Completed in 1574, the Middle Temple Hall is one of the oldest inns of court, and one of the finest Elizabethan halls, in the country. This red-brick building in a Late Gothic style with a double hammerbeam roof was used as a venue for Elizabethan plays, and the first performance of Shakespeare's *Twelfth Night* took place here in 1602.

THE TEMPLE CHURCH

The Temple Church in the Inner Temple was built in the twelfth century by the Knights Templar. This unusual building is the only round church in London, modelled on the Church of the Holy Sepulchre in Jerusalem. Inside, there are splendid effigy tombs of the knights. The Templars' statue situated outside the church is by Nicola Hicks; the two knights sharing a single horse – a symbol of their vows of poverty – is an adaptation of the famous Templar seal.

BLACKFRIAR'S BRIDGE

The first Blackfriar's Bridge, which was designed by Robert Mylne, was completed in 1769. It was originally named Pitt Bridge, but very soon renamed after the Blackfriar Monastery near by. The Portland stone used in the construction soon began to erode and in 1860 the bridge had to be demolished. The new bridge, designed by Joseph Cubitt, was opened by Queen Victoria in 1869. The railway bridge, also designed by Cubitt, was dismantled in 1985 and only the ornate red columns now remain. In 2008, during an annual art exhibtion, it was recreated in lasers as *Ghost Bridge* by Keith Bowler.

OLD CITY OF LONDON SCHOOL

The old City of London School building, currently used by J.P. Morgan, was built by Mowlem and Co. in 1879 in an Italian Renaissance style. The façade is decorated with statues of Shakespeare, Milton, Bacon, Newton and Thomas More, as well as allegorical figures representing the arts and sciences. This building replaced an earlier school of 1835 located in Milk Street. However, the history of the school can be traced back to 1442, when a town clerk bequeathed his estates for the benefit of poor men's children.

UNILEVER HEADQUARTERS

The headquarters of the Anglo-Dutch conglomerate Unilever at 100 Victoria Embankment, completed in 1931, was designed by James Lamax-Simpson, John Barnet and Thomas Tait. It overlaps the north side of the Bridwell Palace built for Henry VIII in 1520. The main crescent elevation has been meticulously restored and the roof area has been significantly improved, providing undisrupted views of St Paul's Cathedral.

THE BLACK FRIAR PUB

The Black Friar stands at the north end of Blackfriars Bridge. It is the only Art Nouveau pub in Central London, built in 1875 on the site of the Blackfriars Monastery. It is famous for its lovely mosaics, both inside and out, and the sculpture of a jolly monk above the main entrance. The pre-Raphaelite murals inside, the work of Henry Pod, create a medieval feel.

CITY DRAGON AT FLEET STREET

In 1880, this dragon replaced the Temple Bar in the middle of Fleet Street. The City dragons guard the entrances and exits of the City. They are symbols of protection and the shield that the dragon statues hold displays the cross of St George and the small red sword of St Paul, the City's patron saint. Fleet Street has been home to the British Press since around 1500, when the very first press was brought here by Wynkyn de Worde. In a short time the street became a meeting place for printers, actors and journalists. The very first newspaper, the *Daily Courant*, was launched here in 1702, and the street became home for many publishers.

PRINCE HENRY'S ROOM

The seventeenth-century Prince Henry's Room at 17 Fleet Street is one of the very few buildings that survived the Great Fire of 1666. It is positioned opposite Sweeney Todd's barber shop, famous for his gruesome practice of killing his customers and making pies of them. The room was used by Prince Henry, Duke of Cornwall, the son of James I. It was said that the promising young prince was 'the best king we never had', as unfortunately an illness cut short his life at the age of eighteen. Currently on display are some prints and paintings of diarist Samuel Pepys (1633–1703).

ST BRIDE'S CHURCH

The current St Bride's is the eighth church to stand on this site. It is known as a church of the press. Printing and publishing businesses were located in Fleet Street for centuries and to this day the church has a strong link with newspaper businesses and journalists. It is instantly recognisable thanks to an amazing spire. The arcaded tiers rise 70 metres high and it is said that the local baker, William Rich, modelled his wedding cakes on Wren's magnificent steeple.

THE MAUGHAN LIBRARY, KING'S COLLEGE LONDON

King's College London is a higher education institute founded by King George IV and the Duke of Wellington in 1829 as an alternative to University College London. The magnificent new library in Chancery Lane, formerly the Public Record Office built by Sir James Pennethorne in 1856, is an outstanding example of neo-gothic architecture.

⚘ MARY QUEEN OF SCOTS HOUSE

The stone statue of Queen Mary on the first-floor façade at 145 Fleet Street, and the spiky tracery of the windows, are Gothic in style. The building was commissioned in the nineteenth century by a patriotic Scottish businessman.

⚘ PETERBOROUGH HOUSE

Elcock, Sutcliffe and Tait's building at 141 Fleet Street was built in 1930. The neoclassical columned façade is made of Portland stone and boasts a lovely Art Deco clock. Formerly used by the *Daily Telegraph*, it is now occupied by Goldman Sachs.

ST DUNSTAN'S-IN-THE-WEST

The church of St Dunstan's-in-the-West on Fleet Street has a famous statue of Queen Elizabeth I situated in the alcove of the church – the only statue of her in London. It dates from 1586 and was the only one carved during her reign. The bracket clock on the church was the first clock in London to be marked with minutes and it was added as a thanksgiving that the old church of 1185 wasn't burned in the Great Fire of 1666. The clock carries two sculptures of the mythical giants Gog and Magog striking the hour with with their clubs.

HOLBORN VIADUCT

Holborn Viaduct is a cast-iron girder bridge linking Holborn
with Newgate Street. It was designed by William Heywood
and completed in 1869. It runs over the subterranean River
Fleet. Two of the four original Renaissance-style houses
that framed the viaduct still exist. The true gems of the
viaduct are the allegorical bronze figures of Commerce,
Agriculture, Science and Fine Art.

STAPLE INN, HIGH HOLBORN

The overhanging black-and-white façade of a half-timbered house called Staple Inn is one of the few surviving Tudor buildings in the City. Built in 1585, it was originally a wool warehouse, hence the name. It remained owned by Woolstaplers until 1580. Later on it became one of the Inns of Chancery. Currently the building is used by the Institute of Actuaries and the lovely street frontage as shops.

CENTRAL CRIMINAL COURT, OLD BAILEY STREET

The lavish neo-baroque building of the Central Criminal Court, commonly known as the Old Bailey, stands on the site of the medieval Newgate Prison, which was demolished in 1902. The court building, designed by Edward Mountford, was completed in 1907. The statue of 'Lady Justice' by Frederick William Pomeroy standing on the dome overlooks the old place of execution. Among the famous trials that took place at the Old Bailey were those of Oscar Wilde and the Yorkshire Ripper. The City of London Corporation maintains the court, and its sherriffs reside permanently at the Old Bailey, their presence underlying the 1,000-year-old tradition of the supervision of law and order.

ST SEPULCHRE-WITHOUT-NEWGATE

This church, at the junction of Holborn Viaduct and Giltspur Street, was founded in 1137. Standing opposite the infamous Newgate Prison, the church bells were used to announce executions. Currently, it is known as a 'musician's church'. There are many famous people buried or commemorated here, including the colourful Elizabethan adventurer Captain John Smith, who sailed to America in 1607, was captured by Native Americans, released by Princess Pocahontas and subsequently became the first Govenor of the State of Virginia.

THE GOLDEN BOY OF PYE CORNER

The Golden Boy was erected on the corner of Giltspur Street and Cock Lane, after the Great Fire of 1666. The inscription underneath reads: 'This boy is in memory put up for the late fire of London, occasioned by the sin of gluttony 1666.' The theory of divine punishment for gluttony was spread by preachers, as the fire started in Pudding Lane. The boy was originally built into the front of a public house, The Fortune of War, whose landlord developed the lucrative but rather grim business of go-between the body snatchers and surgeons from nearby St Bartholomew's Hospital.

ST BARTHOLOMEW'S HOSPITAL

Nicknamed St Bart's, London's oldest hospital was founded by Rahere, a courtier to King Henry I in 1102. It was one of the very few buildings in the City that was not destroyed by the Great Fire. Henry VIII refunded the hospital in 1546 and his statue on the main gate commemorates this event. Set in the North Wing of the hospital is a small museum that chronicles medical history with archives dating back to the twelfth century. The Great Hall contains large murals painted by William Hogarth, one depicting The Good Samaritan, the other Christ at the Pool of Bethesda.

SMITHFIELD MEAT MARKET

Smithfield Meat Market is one of the oldest markets in London, and there was a livestock market on this site as early as the tenth century. The Victorian Grade II listed East and West Buildings, with colourfully painted iron arches, were designed by Sir Horace Jones, who was also the architect of Billingsgate and Leadenhall markets.

WEST SMITHFIELD

This lively area around West Smithfield Garden is situated on a former place of public executions. For more than 400 years people were burned, beheaded or hanged on these grassy fields outside the City walls. It was here that William Wallace was hung, drawn and quartered. A plaque in the wall of St Bartholomew's Hospital commemorates this event. Yet another reminder of gruesome times is the thirteenth-century gateway, topped by a sixteenth-century Elizabethan half-timbered house, where Queen Mary dined while watching Protestants being burned at the stake.

ST BARTHOLOMEW THE GREAT

St Bartholomew the Great is the second oldest church in London. It was founded in 1123 by Henry I's courtier Rahere, whose tomb is in the church and whose ghost, as some swear, occasionally visits the church. The church is the only surviving part of a Norman Priory that was demolished in 1543. Its dark and mysterious interior – in pure Norman style with massive pillars and Romanesque arches – has featured in many films, including *Shakespeare in Love* and *Four Weddings and a Funeral*.

From Barbican to the Millennium Bridge

BARBICAN ESTATE AND ST GILES-WITHOUT-CRIPPLEGATE

The Barbican Estate, developed around the Cripplegate area, was designed by Chamberlain and Bon and built in 1960–73. The heart of the estate is dominated by the Barbican Centre, the largest performing arts centre in Europe. Named for the patron saint of cripples, the medieval church of St Giles was built in 1550. In 1620 Oliver Cromwell was buried here; John Milton was buried here in 1674 and William Shakespeare regularly worshipped here.

THE MUSEUM OF LONDON

The Museum of London was established close to the Barbican Estate in 1975. It is the most comprehensive urban history museum in the world and it shows the history of London through chronological galleries. It contains maps, paintings, weapons, model buildings, coins and other artefects, but the museum's highlight is the Lord Mayor's highly decorative ceremonial coach.

ST BOTOLPH ALDERSGATE, AT MARTIN'S LE GRAND

St Botolph Aldersgate was named after the patron saint of travellers. The present church, with a late-Georgian exterior, was completed in 1791, to the design of Nathaniel Wright. The barrel-vaulted interior of the church has elaborate plasterwork, pannelled columns, wooden galleries and an east window of 1788 with a copy by James Pearson of Corregio's *Agony in the Garden*.

POSTMAN'S PARK

Located between King Edward
Street, Little Britain and Angel
Street, the quiet and shady
Postman's Park takes its name
from its position behind the
former General Post Office. It
was established in 1880 on the
site of the ancient graveyard. The
names of heroic men, women and
children who died attempting to
save others, are commemorated
in over fifty hand-lettered tiles in
a monument by Victorian painter
George Frederick Watts. The
entrance to the park is guarded by
an old police public call post.

ST ANNE AND ST AGNES

The first church on this site was built in Norman times. The only part that survived the Great Fire of 1666 was the tower. The church was rebuilt in 1688 and the tower was incorporated into a building in the shape of a Greek cross. The church was extensively restored in the eighteenth and nineteenth centuries, but suffered serious damage in the Second World War. In the 1960s it was rebuilt according to Christopher Wren's original simple design.

ST JOHN ZACHARY GARDEN

This multi-level garden on the corner of Noble Street and Gresham Street belongs to the Worshipful Company of Goldsmiths. It was established after the Second World War on the site of the old St John Zachary Church that was damaged badly in the Great Fire of 1666. Redesigned in 1996, it is complimented by the adjoining Lloyds TSB building. The south front of this modern building, with its external plant beds, gives an impression of an extension of the vegetation of the garden.

ST ALBAN'S CHURCH

The tower of St Alban's in Wood Street is the only surviving part of this church, built by Sir Christopher Wren in a Perpendicular Gothic style. The rest of the church was destroyed during the Blitz in 1940. The original church, built here in the eighth century by King Offa of Mercia, was replaced in 1634 by a new chuch designed by Inigo Jones and Sir Henry Spiller. Unfortunately this was destroyed by the Great Fire in 1666.

TEMPLE BAR

Reconnecting Paternoster Square with St Paul's Cathedral is Temple Bar, the last surviving City gate. Originally this gate stood on Fleet Street on the border of the City of London and the City of Westminster. The Portland stone arch of 1672, a work of Sir Christopher Wren was commissioned by King Charles II. With growing traffic in the City, it became an obstacle and was removed in 1878. Temple Bar was returned to the City in 2004 and re-erected at Paternoster Square.

➤ GARDENS OF ST MARY ALDERMANBURY

This little garden behind the Guildhall was established on the site of the ruined walls of a Wren church. Plenty of shrubs and other plants create a nice background for a monument to Henry Condell and John Heminges, Shakespeare's friends and partners in the Globe Theatre. They were buried in the churchyard of St Mary Aldermanbury.

PATERNOSTER SQUARE

The prestigious Paternoster Square open-plan piazza, with elegant restaurants, shops and office buildings, is a perfect setting for the neighbouring St Paul's Cathedral. Architects William Whitfield, Richard MacCormac, Eric Parry and others made careful use of Portland stone, granite, marble and York stone to create a restful medium-sized development with a classical feel. The slender Corinthian column with a gilded torch is based on the original design by Inigo Jones for St Paul's Cathedral. The sculpture, at the north end of the square, *Shepherd and Sheep*, is the work of Elisabeth Frink.

BISHOP'S COURT

These sculptural cooling vents in Bishop's Court at the western end of Paternoster Square are the work of Thomas Heatherwick. Underneath this original 11-metre-high stainless steel sculpture is the London electricity substation that powers the whole city.

ST PAUL'S CATHEDRAL

The current cathedral is the fourth to occupy this site.
The first wooden church was erected here in AD 604. The
so-called 'Old St Paul's' was built in 1240, but over the
years it suffered from neglect and deteriorated badly,
before the Great Fire destroyed it completely. The new
cathedral was built by Sir Christopher Wren in 1675–
1710 in a late-Renaissance/baroque style, its dome being
inspired by St Peter's Basilica in Rome. The sculpture
Young Lovers in Festival Gardens on the south side othe
cathedral was designed by George Ehrlich in 1951.

ST MARY LE BOW

St Mary Le Bow church has been at the heart of the community at Cheapside since 1080. It has survived three serious collapses, but the Great Fire destroyed it completely and it was rebuilt by Sir Christopher Wren in 1679. The church is home to the famous Bow Bells, which used to signal a curfew in the City. It is said that to be a true cockney, one has to be born within the sound of these bells. Mary Le Bow was destroyed again in 1941 by a German bomb and only Wren's original crypt survived. The chuch was rebuilt in the 1950s.

'THE LEOPARD',
20 CANNON STREET

This bronze statue, by British sculptor Jonathan Kenworthy, on the corner of Friday Street and Cannon Street, was commissioned by the West Group of companies in 1985. It may be unsual to find a leopard stalking its prey in a city, but it is captvating and strangely fitting in the City's cut-throat environment.

CLEARY GARDENS,
QUEEN VICTORIA STREET

A series of wallked gardens on different levels can be found near Mansion House Tube station. Trees, flowerbeds and climbers are cleverly designed around the ruined Roman walls as well as ruined walls from the bombing in the Second World War.

THE COLLEGE OF ARMS

The Herald's College, or College of Arms, is the official repository of the coats of arms of England, Wales and Northern Ireland. Founded in 1484 by King Richard II, it is a corporate body specialising in genealogical and heraldic work. From 1555 until 1666 the college was based in the medieval Denby Place House on the site of the present college. The current seventeenth-century building was designed by Francis Sandford and Morris Emmett.

THE LONDON MILLENNIUM FOOTBRIDGE

The London Millennium Footbridge is a 320-metre-long wafer-thin pedestrian bridge across the Thames connecting St Paul's Cathedral with Tate Modern. Designed by Sir Norman Foster, it seems to transform into a blade of light in the evenings. When it first opened in 2000 it suffered from a pendulum-like swing and had to be closed. These exciting but rather unwelcome vibrations were eliminated with some modification, but the name 'Wobbly Bridge' stuck.

From Southwark Bridge
to Finsbury Gardens

SOUTHWARK BRIDGE AND VINTNERS' HALL

The current Southwark Bridge was designed by Ernest George and Basil Mott and opened in 1921. The decorative pierced turrets give the bridge a much older appearance than it really is. Near by, overlooking the Thames, stands the oldest livery hall in the City. It was built on the site bequeathed to the Vintners by Guy Shuldham in 1446. The medieval hall burned down in the Great Fire and current one dates from 1671. The company's main role was to regulate the wine trade.

CANNON STREET RAILWAY BRIDGE

This bridge was originally called Princess Alexandra Bridge, after the wife of Edward VIII, Alexandra of Denmark. The bridge and the station were designed by John Hawkshaw and John Wolfe-Barry. Opened in 1866, it was significantly widened in 1886–93 by Francis Brady. The final renovation took place in 1979–92, during which most of the ornament was removed, leaving it functional and simple.

THE LONDON STONE, 111 CANNON STREET

The London Stone is one of London's oldest landmarks. This limestone ancient relict is over 3,000 years old. Previously referred to as the 'Lonestone', it is believed to be part of a pre-Roman altar and, later on, a central milestone of Roman London. One legend claims that it was the London Stone from which Excalibur was pulled by King Arthur. Many people, including Elizabeth I's Merlin, John Dee, believed in its magical powers. The stone was the place of deals, proclamations and important announcements, the passing of laws and swearing of oaths. According to an ancient proverb, 'so long as the stone is safe, so long shall London flourish'.

THE BANK OF ENGLAND

The Bank of England is the central bank of the United Kingdom. It was established in 1694 as a commercial bank to provide William III with finance to fight the French. Acting originally as a government banker, its role evolved over the years. In 1946 it was nationalised and officially became a public central bank. The first building was designed by George Sampson, and wings and the rotunda were added later by Sir Robert Taylor. Sir John Soane succeeded Taylor as the architect and added many halls and courtyards, as well as the massive surrounding curtain wall. Between the two World Wars the building was demolished and a new one by Herbert Baker was erected. The gilded bronze figure on the top of the dome on the corner of Princess Street and Lothbury Street is the symbol of the spirit of the Bank. The statue of the Duke of Wellington in front of the building was cast from the metal of guns taken from the French during the wars.

THE ROYAL EXCHANGE

Adjacent to the Bank of England, the Royal Exchange was founded by Sir Thomas Gresham in 1565. The original building perished in the Great Fire of 1666, and a subsequent building by Edwin Jerman also burned down in 1839. The current, classical building was designed by Sir William Tite and opened in 1844. The London Stock Exchange no longer trades here, but the building, with its lavish covered central courtyard, has been converted into a luxurious shopping centre. At the front is a First World War memorial with two soldiers and a lion, designed by Aston Webb and sculpted by Alfred Drury. The statue behind is of James Henry Greathead (1844–96), the chief engineer of the City and South London Railway.

MANSION HOUSE

At the very heart of the City stands Mansion House, the official residence of the Lord Mayor. It is one of the grandest town palaces, in the Palladian style, with six large Corinthian columns and an impressive pediment ornamented with a group of figures. The house was built in 1739–52 to the design of George Dance the Elder. The Mansion is famous for its 30-metre-long 'Egyptian Hall' and its Art Collection, comprising eighty-four seventeenth-century Dutch and Flemish paintings, bequeathed to the City by Lord Harold Samuel in 1987.

NO. 1 POULTRY

The striped red and cream coloured stone façade of No. 1 Poultry office and retail building has a controversial history. It was designed by James Stirling and completed after twenty years of negotiations. Original plans of Lord Palumbo to build a skyscraper here were rejected and a much smaller building was approved. During construction, some major archaeological discoveries were made, among them a wooden Roman drain.

GEORGE PEABODY, THREADNEEDLE STREET

The statue by William Wetmore Story on the side of the Royal Exchange is of an American philanthropist George Peabody (1795–1869), the first American to be given the freedom of the City of London. An entrepreneur and founder of the Peabody Institute, he settled here in 1837 and donated more than half a million pounds for poor people in London

24–28 LOMBARD STREET

The Royal Insurance Building was designed by the firm of Gordon and Gunton and completed in 1912. The statue above the door is the work of Francis William Doyle-Jones. The female figure on the left depicts the power of the sea, while the figure on the right represents the power of fire. A chimaera with wings in the centre symbolizes the uncertainty of the future.

THE GUILDHALL

The Guildhall is home to the City of London Corporation. The present building, a rare example of medieval civic architecture, was built in 1411–39, but an earlier one was recorded in 1128. Here, royalty and important guests were entertained, large banquets held and famous trials took place. The Guildhall is still used as the place for receptions and banquets for heads of state and other dignitaires. Here also the Lord Mayor is elected every year. It is also used for meetings of the Court of Common Council. The Great Hall, the third largest Civic Hall in England, is over 50 metres long, 16 metres wide and 29 metres high.

GUILDHALL ART GALLERY

Guildhall Art Gallery, designed by Richard Gilbert Scott, stands next to the Great Hall of Guildhall. It was opened in 1999 and replaced an original gallery of 1885 that burned down in an air raid in 1941. The collections in the gallery comprise approximately, 4,000 pieces, mainly British works of art from the seventeenth to the twentieth centuries. It is home of the largest painting in Britain, *The Siege of Gibraltar* by John Copley. Other famous artists represented in the collection are Constable, Millais, Reynolds and Rossetti. In the basement of the gallery, the remains of the Roman amphitheatre discovered in 1988 are displayed.

SHAKESPEARE

LONDON METROPOLITAN UNIVERSITY

London Metropolitan University was created by merging London Guildhall University and the University of North London. The building on Moorgate houses the business school and library. Formerly it housed the headquarters of Cable and Wireless. It was built in a neo-classical style in 1903 by Belcher and Joass.

FINSBURY CIRCUS

The oval garden of Finsbury Circus, surrounded by elegant listed buildings, was designed by Charles Dance the Younger in 1815. It is spread over 2,000 square metres and contains the City of London Bowling Green, a lovely Japanese pagoda and many mature plane trees.

From Broadgate Estate to Tower Hill

BROADGATE ESTATE

Broadgate Estate is a large office and retail development near the old Broad Street Station. Towering above the estate is the 35-storey Broadgate Tower skyscraper. Finsbury Avenue Square is a lovely Italianate piazza with a grid of bright, changing coloured lights designed by Mark Ridler at Maurice Brill Lighting Design. The Broadgate Circle, seemingly based on a Roman arena, is a modern skating and entertainment area encircled by terraces with cafés and restaurants. Nearby Exchange Square is dominated by the 5-ton bronze sculpture *Broadgate Venus* by Fernando Botero.

LIVERPOOL STREET

The bustling Liverpool Street, in the close vicinity of Broadgate Complex is famous for the major railway terminus built in 1875 on the site of the mental hospital of St Mary of Bethlem. The sculpture *Children of the Kindertransport*, by Frank Meisler, situated at the station entrance, commemorates 10,000 children transported to Britain out of the growing Nazi territory.

TURKISH BATH, OLD BROAD STREET

The late-Victorian faux-Islamic Turkish baths opened in 1871, although there were baths here as early as 1817. The present building was designed by Harold Elphic for Henry and James Nevill in 1895. It is topped by an onion dome, which used to hide the water tanks. Closed in 1954, it now houses the Bathhouse Café.

TOWER 42

Tower 42, at 25 Broad Street, was designed by Richard Seifert and originally built by National Westminster Bank in 1979. The footprint of the tower, consisting of three chevrons in a hexagonal arrangement, resembles the logo of the NatWest Bank, but at present Tower 42 is a general-purpose office building. In 1993 an IRA bomb in the Bishopsgate area considerably damaged the building and as a result it was totally reclad with dark glass and stainless steel fins. This pin-strip façade seems to resemble the City's traditional trading outfit.

30 ST MARY AXE

This curvaceous City landmark, affectionately dubbed the 'Gherkin', was designed by Norman Foster to the order of the insurance giant Swiss Re. Providing a sharp contrast to nearby more conventional office blocks, its cigar-like form is the City's first environmentally sustainable tall building.

THE WILLIS BUILDING

The Willis Building at 51 Lime Street was designed by architects Foster & Partners and constructed in 2004–8. The stepped design and the sweeping curve of the building earned it the prestigious New City Architecture Award in 2007. All 3,771 windows of the concave front beautifully reflect the neighbouring buildings. The area at the base of the building has been enlivened by a tree-lined public plaza with attractive cafés, restaurants and shops.

THE LLOYD'S BUILDING

The amazing glass and steel tower of Lloyd's at 1 Lime Street is arguably the most admired modern building in the City. It was designed by Richard Rogers and officially opened by the Queen in 1986. It is 88 metres high and consists of three main towers and three service towers. Described as an 'inside-out' building, it has all the maintenance parts on the outside, thus maximising the available office space. The central open space inside the building is the Underwriting Room, which houses the famous Lutine Bell taken in 1799 from a sunken French ship. This most famous symbol of Lloyd's was traditionally rung to announce important news to underwriters: once for bad news, twice for good news.

LEADENHALL MARKET

The thriving retail centre of Leadenhall Market, off Gracechurch Street, takes its name from the Manor House around which it was etablished. Very quickly it became a favourite place for Londoners to buy meat, poultry, fish and corn. The present market building, with a characteristic iron and glass roof, was designed by Horace Jones in 1881. This beautifully restored Victorian market is a popular place for tourists and city traders to shop and eat.

THE MONUMENT

Known simply as The Monument, this stone column commemorates the Great Fire of 1666, which destroyed thousands of houses, churches and streets. The 61-metre Roman Doric column, topped with a flaming urn of gilt bronze, was designed by Christopher Wren and completed in 1677. Inside, the cantilevered stone staircase consists of 311 steps leading to a viewing platform. The cellar below the ground floor of the column was originally used for physical experiments involving heights.

FISHMONGERS' HALL

The Worshipful Company of Fishmongers was established to regulate the selling of fish and is one of the oldest Livery Companies of the City of London. The current building, at the northern end of London Bridge, dates from 1834, designed in the Greek Revival style by Henry Roberts.

LONDON BRIDGE

The current London Bridge was completed in 1972 and was designed by Mott, Hay and Anderson. This rather plain but functional bridge replaced the so-called 'New London Bridge', built by John Rennie in the nineteenth century, but the most famous bridge here was 'Old London Bridge', by Peter de Colechurch from 1176. It took thirty-three years to build; it had nineteen arches, several homes up to seven storeys high, shops, gatehouses and a drawbridge. Two narrow lanes created traffic and overcrowding problems that frequently resulted in fires. All the houses were removed after the heavy fire of 1758, but this most interesting medieval bridge stood here for an incredible 655 years.

WATERMEN'S HALL

The Watermen's Hall at 16 St Mary-at-Hill was built in 1780 to the design of William Blackburn. It is the only Georgian hall in the City. It was used by the Company of Watermen and Lightermen. In the past, the river played an important role, not only in the transport of goods, but also as a highway for commuters, for cruises and for important civic ceremonies. Every year since 1715, the Watermen have held a rowing race on the Thames, called Doggett's Coat and Badge Race.

OLD BILLINGSGATE MARKET

Billingsgate was London's main port and a general market for coal, corn, salt, fish and other goods. The first fish market was built on the riverside in 1850, but in 1873 was replaced by this beautifully arcaded building designed by Horace Jones. Due to the increased traffic in London, the fish market was moved to the Isle of Dogs in 1982, while this Grade II listed building was converted into a stylish corporate events venue. The blue-mirrored glass façade next to Billingsgate Market is the Northern and Shell Building at No. 10 Lower Thames Street.

GARDENS OF ST DUNSTAN

The ruins of the church on St Dunstan Hill, which was bombed during the Second World War, have been turned into this magical garden with a gothic feel. Climbers on the window frames, water features and immaculate lawns make it a favourite place for a lunch break among busy City works.

MINSTER COURT

Mincing Lane, named after the nuns of St Helen's Bishopsgate, called 'munchens', is home to Minster Court. This modern complex, built in the late 1980s, consists of office buildings in a post-modern gothic style linked by a central-framed glass roof. The building's complexity, its many towers, intricacy of detail and spectacular atria make it an interesting addition to the City skyline.

ALL HALLOWS
BY THE TOWER

Located next to the Tower of London, All Hallows is the oldest church in the City. It was founded by the Saxon Abbey of Barking in AD 675. From the original church, a beautifully preserved arch remains. The church has strong links with the Port of London and seafaring community. All over the church there are models of ships, which are tokens of thanks for safe voyages. It is said that the heart of Richard the Lionheart is buried somewhere in the churchyard.

SEETHING LANE GARDEN

The garden on the corner of Pepys Street and Seething Lane has stong associations with Samuel Pepys. This secluded elongated garden is situated on the site of the Navy Office in which Samuel Pepys, the famous diarist, worked and lived. The building of 1656 escaped the Great Fire, but was demolished in 1788. There is a bust of him among the lovely bushes and mature trees.

10 TRINITY SQUARE

10 Trinity Square is a Grade II listed building designed by Sir Thomas Edwin Cooper and built in 1915–22 as the headquarters of the Port of London Authority. The building has a decorative roof with a statue of Father Thames overlooking the Tower of London. Other statues represent Commerce, Navigation, Exportation and Produce.

TOWER HILL

Tower Hill, Tower Bridge and the Tower of London are not part of the City of London, but are intimately linked with its history. The memorial in front of Trinity House commemorates merchant seamen who died in both World Wars. The 1914–1918 Memorial was designed by Edwin Lutyens and the 1939–1945 Memorial by Sir Edward Maufe. To the east of both memorials, overlooking the Tower of London, is a delightful sundial with an anchor and chain, the work of John Chitty.

TOWER OF LONDON

Officially known as Her Majesty's Royal Palace and Fortress, steeped in history and mystery, the Tower of London was built around 1077 by William the Conqueror on the north bank of the Thames to assert his power and to keep an eye on the city. Successive monarchs enlarged the Tower and added buildings, towers and walkways, as well as defensive walls, transforming it into a magnificent fortress.

TOWER BRIDGE

One London's most famous landmarks, Tower Bridge was completed in 1894. Designed by Horace Jones, it is a combination of a suspension bridge and a bascule bridge, an engineering marvel at the time, which allowed the passage of tall ships into the Port of London. The lower road is made up of two halves, which used to be raised by hydraulic bascules powered by steam; nowadays they are oil and electricity powered.

Index